SPLITTING

AND DAGENHAM

by Karen Bryant-Mole

Consultant: John Hall,
Counselling Support Manager of ChildLine

Adoption

Bullying

Child Abuse

Death

Growing Up

Splitting Up

Step Families

Designed by Helen White
Edited by Deb Elliott

We gratefully acknowledge the assistance of the following people
in the production of this book:
Dr Rachel Waugh, Principal Clinical Psychologist,
Great Ormond Street Hospital

All the words in **bold** are explained in the glossary on page 31.

This edition published in 1994 by Wayland (Publishers) Ltd

First published in 1992 by Wayland (Publishers) Limited
61 Western Road, Hove, East Sussex BN3 1JD

British Library Cataloguing in Publication Data
Bryant – Mole, Karen
  Splitting Up. – (What's Happening? Series)
  I. Title II. Series
  306.89

HARDBACK ISBN 0-7502-0397-8

PAPERBACK ISBN 0-7502-1380-9

Phototypeset by White Design
Printed and bound in Italy by G. Canale & C. S. p. A.

CONTENTS

Families 4

It's No One's Fault 6

Feelings 8

Living Arrangements 10

The Conciliator 12

Sorting Things Out 14

Changes 16

Talking About It 18

Jane 20

Tom 22

Visits 24

New Partners 26

Things Get Better 28

For Parents and Teachers 30

Glossary 31

Books To Read 31

Index 32

FAMILIES

Look at all the people on the beach in the photograph opposite. Many of them are families, but do you think they are all the same type of family?

Sarah lives with both her mum and her dad. Paul and Jim live with just their mum. Kate and Sam live with their dad, his new wife Angie, and her two children, Tom and Chris. Gary lives with his mum, dad, granny, grandad and lots of pets! They all live in families but all the families are different.

Sometimes, when parents split up, children feel that they aren't a proper family any more. Things might change, perhaps the mum or dad will move out of the house, but families are about much more than where people live. Families are about people loving and caring for each other. That doesn't have to change at all.

OPPOSITE Families come in all shapes and sizes.

BELOW Families aren't just about who you live with, they are about people caring for each other.

IT'S NO ONE'S FAULT

ABOVE Friendships often change as you grow older.

If a mum and dad split up, children often try to think of a reason why this is happening. Some children decide that it's all their fault. Sometimes they think that it's because they haven't been good enough.

Most parents split up because of problems between themselves, not because of problems between them and their children. It can be difficult to understand, but in the same way that you fall out with your friends at school, adults fall out with each other too. Think back to when you first went to school. Do you still have exactly the same friends now as you did then? Why not? Perhaps they are interested in things that you aren't.

They might have changed in other ways. No one stays the same for ever, not even adults. Your parents may feel that instead of being best friends, they really aren't very good friends at all now.

Sometimes children who think that it's their fault when their parents split up decide to be extra good, hoping it will make everything all right again. They try as hard as they can to do things that will please their parents, but as that isn't the reason why their parents are splitting up it probably won't keep them together.

LEFT Being good is unlikely to bring your mum and dad back together, but they will probably be grateful for your help.

FEELINGS

Philip feels that the worst bit about his mum and dad splitting up was that it made them cry. He had never seen them cry before. He thought parents were only supposed to look after children when they cried.

It might help you to understand why Philip's mum and dad cried if you think about the way you feel. You probably feel upset that your parents are splitting up. You might feel you want to cry. You might even feel very angry about it. Adults have feelings like this too and sometimes it makes them cry if they are upset or shout if they are angry.

BELOW It can be very upsetting to hear people crying or arguing, especially at night

Gemma's parents used to argue a lot and she hated it. She especially didn't like it when they argued at night. She used to lie in bed with her fingers in her ears so she couldn't hear the shouting. She wanted to yell out 'Stop it!' at the top of her voice. It was very frightening.

If you are frightened by arguing or upset by crying, try to talk to your mum and dad about it. They probably don't want to hurt you and may not realize how scary their arguments sound to someone else.

ABOVE Try talking to your mum and dad and letting them know how frightening you find it when they argue.

9

LIVING ARRANGEMENTS

ABOVE Siew and Mai Lin live with their dad but often stay with their mum.

One of the first things that many children think about when they realize that their parents may be splitting up is *'What's going to happen to me?'* They want to know where they are going to live and who they are going to live with.

When Siew and Mai Lin's parents split up they sold their house. Their mum bought a flat and the girls now live with their dad in a smaller house. This seemed to be the best **arrangement** for everyone. Their mum is a doctor and often works at nights. Their dad is an architect. He works for himself and can work hours that fit in with the school day and always be with the girls at night. Even though Siew and Mai Lin don't live with their mum any more they still see her as much as possible and often stay at her flat when she isn't on night duty.

For Jon it was better the other way round. His dad was a long-distance lorry driver and was often away for days at a time, while his mum had a part-time job in a supermarket. So Jon stayed with his mum. That didn't mean that his dad didn't love him or didn't want him, it was just that he wouldn't have been able to look after Jon in the way that he would want to.

No two situations are exactly the same. Where you live and who you live with will depend on lots of different things but your parents should always think about what's best for you.

BELOW There are lots of things to think about when deciding where it would be best for you to live.

THE CONCILIATOR

ABOVE *Your parents might visit a conciliator.*

When Lucy's mum and dad split up they both said they wanted Lucy to live with them. They couldn't agree about what would be best for her so they decided to go to see someone called a **conciliator**. A conciliator is a person who helps people sort out many of the things they disagree about.

Sometimes it can be very difficult for people to sort out things themselves. Have you ever had an argument with anyone? Jo and Rory were fighting over a tennis racquet and ball. Rory wanted a go but Jo said that she was going to play with them all playtime. A teacher came over. She didn't make Jo hand over the racquet and ball to Rory. Instead she asked them to think about how they could solve the argument in a way that was as fair as possible. They talked about it and decided that if they got another racquet not only could they both play but it would be much better than playing by themselves.

Jo and Rory's teacher was like a conciliator. She didn't tell them what to do. She listened to the problem and helped them to talk about it and sort it out.

If she hadn't been there they would have spent the rest of playtime arguing and would have gone back into class feeling very cross with one another. Neither Jo nor Rory got exactly what they had wanted at first but they reached an agreement that they were both happy with. In the same sort of way a conciliator can help parents sort things out as fairly as possible.

BELOW You could be asked by the conciliator and your parents to say how you feel.

SORTING THINGS OUT

Sometimes parents can't agree about what will be best for their children even with the help of a conciliator, so a **judge** in a court decides for them. The most important person to the judge is you!

If this happens to you, you will probably meet someone called a **court welfare officer**. He or she will talk to you and your parents. If you want to, you can tell the court welfare officer what you would like to happen. If you don't know, that's all right too. The court welfare officer isn't trying to make you choose between your parents, he or she is only trying to find out what might be best for you.

In the court the judge will listen to what your parents and the court welfare officer have to say. The judge will decide what arrangements are best for you.

The arrangements made by the judge will use words that you might not understand. '**Residence orders**' are to do with where you will live. '**Contact orders**' are to do with things like meeting, visiting and phoning the parent that you don't live with.

Everyone's residence and contact orders will be different. The judge will always try to make sure that you see as much of both parents as you would like and that they both continue to be part of your life.

OPPOSITE The court welfare officer will try to find out what might be best for you. Going to court doesn't mean that anyone has been bad.

CHANGES

A lot of children feel very confused when their parents are splitting up.

Every weekday used to be the same for Laura. She had breakfast with her mum and dad, went to school, came home, watched television, had tea, played outside, had a bath and went to bed. Suddenly everything changed. Sometimes her dad wasn't at breakfast. Sometimes she had to go to friends' houses after school. When she was told that her mum and dad were splitting up she felt even more muddled up. If mum and dad didn't love each other any more, perhaps they didn't love her any more either. Perhaps they had never loved her.

BELOW Some things stay the same even when everything else around you is changing.

LEFT Laura still plays basketball on Saturdays.

When things are changing all around you it is easy to feel confused. Your mum and dad are probably the two most important people in your life so it is natural to feel worried about what is happening.

Laura found going to school helpful. At school the right things still happened at the right times. Her friends were just the same too.

Like Laura, lots of children worry about whether or not their parents still love them. It is very important to remember that it is not you your parents are splitting up from, it is each other. Even if they can't get along together any more your mum and your dad will both always love you.

TALKING ABOUT IT

If you feel confused about what is going on, it might help to talk to someone about it. If it is difficult to talk to your parents about it, try talking to your grandparents or a teacher. There were lots of things that Daniel wanted to talk about when his parents split up.

One day when he was at his grandmother's he fell over and cut his leg. It was only a little cut but he couldn't stop crying. His grandmother gave him a cuddle. Suddenly Daniel found himself saying all the things he had wanted to say to his mum and dad. Why did it have to happen to his family? Why couldn't they just be friends again? He told his grandmother that sometimes he felt angry with his mum and dad, sometimes he felt frightened and sometimes he just felt sad.

Daniel's grandmother cuddled him and listened. She didn't give him any answers and she didn't make any promises, she just listened. When Daniel stopped talking he felt much better. All the thoughts and questions had been buzzing around inside him for so long that they had become a mess. Saying them out loud had somehow sorted the mess out a little bit.

OPPOSITE You might find that talking helps. If it is a bit difficult to talk to adults about the way you feel, try thinking about what you would like to say before actually talking to them.

JANE

This is Jane's story about her parents splitting up.

'My mum and dad always seemed to be arguing. When I asked them why they said it was nothing to do with me. In the end they hardly talked at all. One day I came home from school and all dad's things had gone. Mum said he had gone to live somewhere else because he didn't like us any more. She said we would be better off without him. She said all sorts of horrid things about my dad but I really missed him.

'A few weeks later mum said that dad was going to take me out for the day. I was really excited but it all went wrong. Dad turned up and the first thing they did was have a row on the doorstep where all the neighbours could hear. Dad wanted to take me swimming but mum said I had a cold and couldn't go. Mum wanted me home for tea but dad said he wanted to take me for a burger. No one asked me what I wanted.

'Dad kept spoiling the day by talking about mum in a nasty way and saying that it was all her fault we weren't together any more. The day finished off with another argument. Dad brought me back ten minutes late.

Mum was absolutely furious. I just ran upstairs and shut myself in my bedroom.

'All I wanted was for them to be nice to each other. I knew they didn't love each other any more but I still loved both of them.'

Jane's parents were so cross and angry with each other that they only thought about themselves and not about her. How do you think they could have made things easier for Jane?

LEFT No one thought about how Jane was feeling.

TOM

ABOVE Tom used to cry when he thought about his parents splitting up.

This is what happened to Tom when his parents split up.

'I knew things weren't going too well at home. I asked dad what was wrong and he said perhaps we had all better talk about it. The next day he came home early from work. I felt a bit funny, like I knew I was going to hear some bad news. Mum said that she and dad didn't think they could keep on living together in the same house any more. It was making them both unhappy. I started to cry and dad gave me a big hug.

'Dad said that he and mum had talked about it a lot and thought about what would be best for my little sister and me. He said that mum and me and my sister could stay in the house and that he would move into a flat not far away. They asked me what I thought about it but all I could say was that I wanted to live with both of them. I didn't want dad to move out.

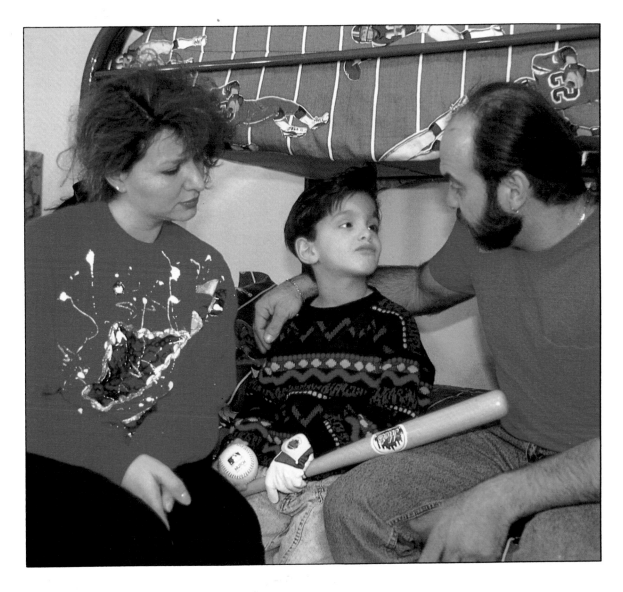

'After that we didn't talk about it for a couple of days but I kept thinking about it all the time. One night I couldn't get to sleep. Mum and dad asked me if I wanted to talk about it. I told them all the things I was worried about. Dad said that even though some things might change, he and mum were both still my parents and they would always love me and look after me. I was very sad about it but at least I felt that I wouldn't be losing dad.'

ABOVE Tom found it helpful to know that he could talk to his parents and that they would listen.

VISITS

After your parents have split up you will probably live with one parent for most of the time and visit the other parent. Visiting someone you used to live with might feel a bit strange at first. It will probably feel strange to your mum and dad too. You might not know what to say to each other or how to behave. You might wonder whether or not you should talk about the other parent, but that doesn't mean you have to love one and not the other. It's all right for you to love both of them.

Sometimes the person that you visit feels that they have got to make it up to you because they don't see you all the time. They might buy you lots of presents or take you to really exciting places.

Jamie lived with his mum during the week and visited his dad every other weekend. When he went back to his mum his dad always gave him a present. Jamie didn't really need all those presents but he did like them. The trouble was that whenever Jamie got cross with his mum he started to say things like *'I like dad better than you because he buys me presents'*, and *'I don't want to live with you any more because we never do anything exciting.'* Do you think Jamie was being fair to his mum?

OPPOSITE *You don't have to choose between your parents. You can still love both of them. It is all right to enjoy being with both of them.*

NEW PARTNERS

Sometimes after a mum and dad have split up they get a new boyfriend or girlfriend. If that happens you might not be quite sure whether you feel pleased or upset.

Abby thought it was great when her dad got a new girlfriend because she had been anxious about him being lonely. His girlfriend was good fun too and Abby got on really well with her. Sometimes she worried about it though. She wasn't sure how liking her dad's girlfriend would make her mum feel. So when she talked about her to her mum she used to say things such as *'She's not as pretty as you mum'*. This was so her mum wouldn't think that Abby liked the new girlfriend better than her.

BELOW Meeting a parent's new boyfriend or girlfriend can feel a bit strange.

Scott hated it when his mum got a new boyfriend. Since his dad had left he felt that he had been the one who looked after his mum. Now this other person was trying to take over. His mum didn't need anyone else, she had him. Scott didn't like the boyfriend telling him what to do either. He wasn't his dad, so how dare he tell him what to do.

BELOW Whether or not they have new boyfriends or girl-friends, your mum will always be your mum and your dad will always be your dad.

If there is a new boyfriend or girlfriend it will seem strange to everyone for a while, even to your mum or dad. You may not be sure how you feel about it and they will probably find it a bit uncomfortable at first too. It will take time for you all to get to know each other and to sort out a way of getting on together.

THINGS GET BETTER

If your mum and dad are splitting up you might be feeling pretty miserable about it right now. But things usually do get better even though sometimes it might seem to take for ever.

These children all have parents who have **separated** and this is how they feel about it now.

'Before my mum and dad split up they were always rowing. I didn't like it. I didn't want my friends to come to my house in case my mum and dad had an argument when they were there. At first I was sad when mum left but now I think it was the best thing to do. Mum and dad are both much happier and so am I. It's nice to know that when I come home from school they won't be shouting at each other or crying.'

'I didn't want mum and dad to split up. I couldn't understand why dad wanted to leave me and my sister. Because of the way things turned out I hardly ever see him any more. I used to mind about it a lot, but I've got used to it now. My mum and sister and me get on really well together.'

'When my mum and dad split up I thought I was the unhappiest person on earth. I thought that I would never have a nice time ever again. I felt like this for quite a long time. Then I started to get used to our new life and in lots of ways I like it better. Lots of things have changed but I still see both my mum and dad. I know they both love me and that's the most important thing of all.'

FOR PARENTS AND TEACHERS

No one can offer you hard and fast rules about the 'best' way to help a child through a separation but here are a few guidelines that you may find useful.

- Encourage the child to express his or her fears and feelings. Some children cope with a separation by refusing to think or talk about it. This is not helpful in the long term.

- Listen to the child and ask what he or she wants too. Answer questions but don't make any promises that you can't keep or which are outside your control.

- Be honest with the child and keep him or her informed and involved. Know too when to stop. Hearing all the ins and outs of events preceding a separation may not be of benefit to the child.

- Remember the needs of the child. It is easy to get so wrapped up in your own problems that you overlook his or her needs.

- Try to keep life as normal as possible. In a time of change, everyday events, such as friends coming home for tea and even ensuring that house rules are kept, provide a much needed anchor.

- Try to be civil with and about your ex-partner. Acrimony between parents is one of the things that children who have been through a separation say they found very distressing.

- Give the child time to come to terms with any new relationship you begin and don't expect him or her to be as happy about it as you are.

- Children can and do emerge from a separation both happy and well-adjusted. Your attitude and actions as parents and teachers will profoundly influence the way the separation affects the child.

GLOSSARY

Arrangement An agreement or plan that people make together.

Conciliator A person whose job it is to help people sort out arguments or disagreements.

Contact orders Arrangements made in a court which say when the parent who the child is living with should allow the other parent to visit, meet and phone the child.

Court A place where decisions and judgements are made.

Court welfare officer A person chosen by the court who talks to the parents and the children to help work out what is best for the children.

Judge The person who hears cases in a court and decides what action, if any, should be taken.

Residence orders Arrangement made by a judge in court which say where children should live if their parents split up.

Separated When parents live apart.

BOOKS TO READ

Children Don't Divorce by Rosemary Stones (Harper Collins, 1992)
Children Need Families by Michael Pollard (Wayland, 1988)
Dinosaurs Divorce by L.K. Brown and Marc Brown (Collins, 1987)
Divorce by Liz Friedrich (Gloucester Press, 1988)
How It Feels When Parents Divorce by Jill Krementz (Victor Gollancz, 1985)
Step Families by Karen Bryant-Mole (Wayland, 1993)
Step Families by Angela Grunsell (Gloucester Press, 1990)
Your Family by Michael Pollard (Wayland, 1989)

INDEX

Arguments 9, 20, 27

Changes 16, 17, 22, 29
Conciliator 12, 13, 14
Contact orders 14
Court 14
Court welfare officer 14
Crying 8, 9, 18, 22, 28

Falling out 6
Families 4
Feelings 8, 9, 21
Friends 6, 7, 17, 28

Judge 14

Living arrangements 10, 11, 14

New partners 26, 27

Residence orders 14

School 6, 7, 28

Visits 14, 24

Picture Acknowledgements

The following pictures are from: Eye Ubiquitous 11, 20; Jeff Greenberg 4, 6, 7, 8, 9, 16, 17, 22, 23, 26, 27; Zul Mukhida/Chapel Studios 12, 13, 15, 19; Tony Stone Worldwide cover, 5; Wayland Picture Library 10, 21, 28, 29; Some of the people who are featured in the photographs in this book are models. We gratefully acknowledge the help and co-operation of all those individuals who have been involved in this project.